Impact on Earth

The Impact of
PLASTICS

Ruth Daly

Crabtree Publishing Company
www.crabtreebooks.com

CRABTREE
PUBLISHING COMPANY
WWW.CRABTREEBOOKS.COM

Author: Ruth Daly

Editorial director: Kathy Middleton

Editor: Ellen Rodger

Picture Manager: Sophie Mortimer

Design Manager: Keith Davis

Children's Publisher: Anne O'Daly

Production coordinator and prepress: Ken Wright

Print coordinator: Katherine Berti

Photo credits
(t=top, b= bottom, l=left, r=right, c=center)

Front Cover: All images from Shutterstock

Interior: iStock: Koldunov; Public Domain: Open Access, MIT/ Digital 23, Monmarad.gov.mn 13; Shutterstock: Mohamed Abdulraheem 16, Africa Studio 28 Rich Carey 12, 18, Chiociolla 9, clicksabhi 22, Meale Cousland 7, Mike dotta 26, Elena Elisseeva 11, Elizaveta Galitckaia 20, Tome Grundy 17, Vladislav T. Jirousek 19, Anan Kaewkhammuk 5, Anjo Kan 25, Sebastian Knight 27, Ana Kumka 4, Larina Marina 8, nicemyphoto 21, SewCream 29, Stock 15, wavebreakmedia 6.

Library and Archives Canada Cataloguing in Publication

Title: The impact of plastics / Ruth Daly.
Names: Daly, Ruth, 1962- author.
Description: Series statement: Impact on Earth | Includes index.
Identifiers: Canadiana (print) 20200165852 |
  Canadiana (ebook) 20200165860 |
  ISBN 9780778774372 (hardcover) |
  ISBN 9780778774631 (softcover) |
  ISBN 9781427125163 (HTML)
Subjects: LCSH: Plastic scrap—Environmental aspects—Juvenile
  literature. | LCSH: Plastics—Environmental aspects—Juvenile
  literature. | LCSH: Plastic scrap—Juvenile literature. |
  LCSH: Plastics—Juvenile literature.
Classification: LCC TD798 .D35 2020 | DDC j363.72/88—dc23

Library of Congress Cataloging-in-Publication Data

CIP available at the Library of Congress

LCCN: 2019058744

Printed in the U.S.A./022020/CG20200102

Published in Canada
Crabtree Publishing
616 Welland Avenue
St. Catharines, ON
L2M 5V6

Published in the United States
Crabtree Publishing
PMB 59051
350 Fifth Ave, 59th Floor
New York, NY 10118

Contents

What Is Plastic?

Plastic is a material used to make many things. You'll find it in a lot of items, from toothbrushes to washing machines to toys.

Plastic is a human-made material. Modern plastic was invented by a Belgian chemist named Leo Baekeland. Today there are more than 50 kinds of plastics. Cellophane is a thin, transparent sheet of plastic, used for wrapping packages. Stretchy nylon is often used in fibers for clothing. Polystyrene, or Styrofoam, is commonly used in food packaging.

Plastic can be colored and it can be hard or soft. It is used to make all sorts of household products, including food storage containers.

Plastic and Fossil Fuels

Almost all plastics are made from chemicals that come from **fossil fuels** such as oil. When they are burned, these fuels produce **greenhouse gases** that harm the environment by trapping heat near Earth. **Reducing** our use of both plastics and fossil fuels is a first step in helping the planet.

1907 Year modern plastic was invented

1970s Decade plastic grocery bags were introduced

Long Lasting

Plastic is strong and lasts a long time. It can be formed into different shapes. More than 9 billion tons (8 billion metric tons) of plastic have been produced since the 1950s. Plastic does not **decompose** quickly. In fact, all the plastic ever made is still somewhere on Earth. That's a problem.

Many Uses of Plastics

Each kind of plastic has different **properties** that make it suited to a specific use. You will see plastic in many places. It is used in vehicles, farm machinery, and smaller items such as stir sticks and glitter. There are plastic signs to give us directions, plastic chairs to sit on, and even plastic bills for money! In stores, plastic containers hold ice cream, juice, and soup. Plastic bags keep fruit and bread fresh longer.

Plastic is used to make artificial limbs because it is strong, light, and flexible. Some artifical limbs are specially designed for sports.

Plastic Money

Plastic bills are made from thin plastic film called polymer. Plastic bills last longer than paper ones. They don't get wet and dirty and are harder to fake. First used in Australia in 1988, more than 20 other countries now use plastic bills, including Canada, New Zealand, and the United Kingdom. At present, the United States still uses paper bills.

300 million tons (270 million metric tons)
Amount of plastic produced each year

2011 Year plastic bills were first used in Canada

Good and Bad

Plastic has uses that improve the quality of life and even saves lives. It is used to make artificial limbs and child-proof lids on medicine bottles. In hospitals, plastic gloves help prevent the spread of disease. Plastic containers are cheaper than glass. On the other hand, it is much easier to **recycle** glass and metal. The problem with plastic materials is that only some kinds of plastic can be recycled.

Why Worry?

Plastic does not easily break down. Although it breaks into smaller pieces, it is never completely gone.

Some plastics are designed to be used only once. These are called single-use plastics, and they make up about 40 percent of all plastic **waste**. Single-use plastics include drinking straws, stir sticks, and grocery bags. They are cheap and convenient. We often use them once and throw them out.

A plastic bottle takes 1,000 years to decompose. It leaks toxic chemicals into the environment as it does so.

Swap Your Plastic

Make a plan to stop buying single-use plastics. Use products that can be used many times, such as metal straws instead of plastic ones. Use a bar of soap for your shower instead of shower gel in a bottle. Trade your plastic toothbrush for a bamboo toothbrush. Take a cotton tote bag to the store instead of buying a plastic bag.

50% Percentage of plastic produced each year used for single-use items

5 trillion Number of single-use plastic bags used globally every year

Plastic Pollution

Plastic waste **pollutes** the environment. **Toxic** materials inside the plastic get into the soil or water. Farmland and rivers become polluted. Sometimes plastic waste is destroyed by incineration, or burning. This releases **carbon dioxide** into the atmosphere, contributing to the buildup of greenhouse gases.

Microplastics

Microplastics are tiny pieces of plastic that are about the size of a grain of rice. Some pieces start small. They come from clothing fibers, cosmetics, and nurdles, which are small plastic pellets. Others start as larger pieces of plastic that break up into smaller pieces. Microplastics can be found in paint chips that scrape off the sides of boats and in the dust that tires leave on the road.

Glitter is a microplastic. It might look pretty in craft projects and cosmetics, but it is dangerous to sea animals that eat it.

Check What You Wear

Check the labels when you're buying clothes. Look for natural fibers such as wool and cotton. All clothes shed tiny fibers in the wash, but natural fibers break down easily. Human-made fibers, such as nylon and polyester, take much longer to break down.

More than 8 trillion
Number of microbeads released into water supply in U.S.A. each day

About 100,000 Number of
microbeads released in a single shower

Tiny but Terrible

Microbeads are even smaller than microplastics. These tiny pieces of plastic are less than 0.04 inches (1 mm) in size. They act as scrubbers in some toothpastes, soaps, and face creams. Once used, they are washed into the drains and into our water supply. Microbeads absorb other materials easily, including toxic substances.

Plastics in the Ocean

Plastic gets into the sea when garbage blows into rivers. It is carried to the ocean where currents take it farther out.

Boats, cargo ships, and off-shore oil rigs add to the problem. Fishing nets are lost, garbage is tossed overboard, and cargo can be lost in stormy weather. The result is that each of the world's five oceans has its own huge garbage patch.

Around two thirds of the plastic in the oceans comes from land sources. This includes garbage left on beaches and washed down rivers and drains.

Great Pacific Garbage Patch

The biggest ocean garbage patch is the Great Pacific Garbage Patch. Located in the Pacific Ocean between Hawaii and California, it is about two times as large as Texas. Scientists think there could be from 1.1 million to 3.6 million plastic pieces in the Great Pacific Garbage Patch.

8.8 million tons (8 million metric tons)
Amount of plastic in the ocean

70% Percentage of garbage in the ocean that sinks to the bottom

Deep, Dark Sea

Sunlight breaks plastic into smaller pieces. This is called photodegradation. In the ocean, most of the plastic sinks to the seafloor where it is dark. Sunlight cannot reach there, and plastic takes longer to decompose. Plastic bags take 10 years to decompose in the ocean. Sandwich bags take 1,000 years.

Plastics on the Coast

The beach is no place for plastic garbage but people sometimes leave it there. Other plastic comes onto the beach with the tides. Some plastic garbage is carried by rivers to the coast where it washes up on the shore. All garbage is harmful to beaches. Plastic garbage is particularly toxic. Some microplastics are too small to be seen. They are eaten or inhaled by marine life and people.

Plastic trash covers a beach in Bali. The island is popular with tourists. It has banned plastic bags, straws, and Styrofoam to cut down plastic waste.

Taking Action

People have been taking action. Each year, thousands of volunteers join beach cleanups. They pick up trash from their local beaches. The biggest cleanup is arranged each year by Ocean Conservancy. It organizes cleanups all around the world. Since it began 30 years ago, volunteers have removed 300 million pounds (136 million kg) of garbage from about 500,000 miles (800,000 km) of beach!

More than 12 million Number of volunteers from 153 countries who have joined in Ocean Conservancy's beach cleanups

20% Percentage of plastic in Bali's total waste

WHAT CAN I DO?

Join a Beach Cleanup!

If you live near a shoreline, join a beach cleanup. Cleanups are advertised on social media. They help to make beaches clean and safer for humans and wildlife. They're fun, too! Go with friends or family. Every piece of plastic you collect is one step closer to a plastic-free ocean!

Plastics and Wildlife

Plastic trash is killing wildlife. Marine animals get stuck in plastic nets or eat plastic that they think is food.

Plastic has been found in 60 percent of seabirds. It blocks their digestive system. The birds feel full, but their stomachs are filled with plastic not food. The birds don't eat so they starve to death. Albatrosses have fed small plastic pellets to their chicks because the pellets look like fish eggs.

Marine animals such as sea turtles get tangled in lost and abandoned fishing nets. Hundreds of animals can get caught in one net.

Write a Letter

Making people aware of the urgent situation is an important part in the fight against plastic pollution. Write a letter to your local newspaper about how plastic ends up in oceans and how it impacts marine wildlife.

46% Percentage of the Great Pacific Garbage Patch that is ghost nets

More than 700 Number of species of marine animals that have eaten or become entangled in plastic

Ghost Nets

Ghost nets are plastic fishing nets that are no longer used. They have been left in the ocean by fishers. Marine animals get tangled in the nets and are injured. If they cannot free themselves, they can drown. The nets break down into smaller pieces. This adds to the microplastics that are in the ocean.

Oxygen Makers

Plankton and **algae** are tiny organisms that grow in oceans and other water bodies. They are the main food source for many small marine animals. Plankton and algae also make most of the world's oxygen, but they need sunlight to do this. Garbage patches form a barrier between the Sun and the algae and plankton. This makes it impossible for these organisms to grow and produce oxygen.

Whale sharks are the world's biggest fish, yet they feed on tiny plankton. Scientists think these fish could be swallowing hundreds of pieces of plastic a day.

Marine Mammals

Whales, dolphins, and seals are mammals. Although they live in water, they cannot breathe underwater. If they get caught up in nets, they drown. These animals feed their young on milk. When they eat fish that have plastic in their bodies, the plastic gets passed onto their young through the mothers' milk.

100 million Number of mammals killed each year by plastic pollution

93% Percentage of bottled water that contains microplastics

Where Has All the Food Gone?

Less algae means less food for small sea creatures to eat. The entire **food chain** is affected by this, resulting in fewer turtles and fish, which means less food for sharks and whales. Eventually this impacts humans, especially those who eat seafood. Plastic in the fish can become part of our food, too. Microplastics have also been found in tap water and bottled water.

Reducing Plastic Use

The best way for us to reduce plastic waste is to make lifestyle changes. One way is to take better care of the plastic items we already have.

Taking care of electronics, games, and toys helps them last longer. We do not have to replace them as often. Find creative ways to **reuse** some of your plastic containers. Instead of throwing them out, you could use them for storing pens or coins.

Banana leaves are a natural alternative to plastic. They can be used as plates and for serving and wrapping food.

Plastic-Free Parties

Try having a plastic-free birthday! Avoid using plastic plates, cups, and cutlery. Instead of using plastic straws, use no straws at all. Use reusable treat bags so your friends can use them later. Fill the bags with homemade cookies or environmentally friendly items such as sunflower seeds to plant or bird seed.

500 million Number of plastic straws used in U.S.A. every day

2050 Year by which there will be more plastic in the ocean than fish

Natural Alternatives

The next time you run out of something plastic, replace it with something made out of metal, glass, or wood. Buy a metal water bottle that can be washed and refilled. Try glass storage jars instead of plastic ones. Use a wooden cutting board in the kitchen. These will last longer, and they are better for the environment, too.

Plastic Recycling

Recycling is the practice of making waste materials into something new. Different types of plastics are made with different ingredients. Only some kinds can be recycled. Check the label on plastic items to see if they can be recycled. Many neighborhoods have recycling programs, but they don't take all kinds of plastic. Some recycling programs do not accept bottle caps or plastic toys. Look up the rules where you live to see which items can be recycled.

A boy collects plastic bottles from a garbage dump in India to sell. About 15 million people around the world sort through trash like this to try to make enough money to live.

Robots Recycle

Recycled waste has to be sorted into different groups. This work is done by people. It is dirty and dull and can be dangerous. Scientists have invented a robot called RoCycle that has a special "hand." It has sensors that can tell if an item is plastic, metal, or paper.

1 million Number of plastic bottles bought every minute

Less than half Number of those bottles recycled

Sending Recycling Overseas

Some countries send their plastic waste to other countries to be recycled. If the plastic is dirty or mixed with non-recyclable waste, it ends up in a **landfill**, or dump, and pollutes the local environment. Some countries have stopped taking in plastic waste. Imports of plastic waste were banned by China in 2018 and India in 2019.

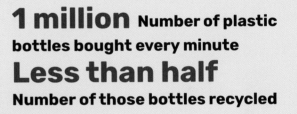

Future Developments

Sunglasses, sneakers, lawn chairs, carpet fibers, and recycling bins can all be made from recycled plastics.

Recycled plastic bottles can be made into t-shirts, sleeping bags, and padding for ski jackets. Plastic bags can be recycled into playground equipment. Bottle caps are turned into garden rakes. A company in California makes sunglasses from recycled plastic fishing nets. It gives some of the money it makes to help coastal communities that are affected by plastic pollution.

These colorful bags are made from recycled plastic. Buying items made from recycled plastic keeps waste from going into landfills and the oceans.

Helping Refugees

In 2016, 850,000 **refugees** arrived by sea on Greece's shores looking for a safer life. Thousands of life vests washed up on the beaches. A Dutch organization called Makers Unite took 5,000 life vests to Amsterdam. There, refugees turned the life vests into new products, including bags and laptop holders. The money from the sale of the bags goes to help refugee projects.

2002 Year Bangladesh banned plastic grocery bags

2008 Year Rwanda banned plastic that does not biodegrade

Governments Take Action

In 2019, around 180 countries signed an agreement to reduce the amount of plastic that ends up in the oceans. Governments can help by banning single-use plastics. In Africa, 25 countries have banned plastic bags. Australia and India have laws to make plastic producers more responsible for recycling their products.

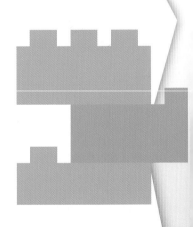

Plant-based plastics are being used to make fast-food glasses, cups, cutlery, and food boxes.

Clean Plastics

Scientists are developing new types of plastic that are less harmful to the environment. **Bioplastics** are made from plants like sugarcane and corn instead of from fossil fuels. They are used to make packaging for food, bottles, and utensils. Clothing can be made from bioplastics, and they are used to make some medical equipment. When bioplastics break down, they release less carbon into the atmosphere than oil-based plastics.

Bioplastic Waste

Bioplastics are not without problems. They must be heated to very high temperatures to break down. If they end up in landfills and the ocean, they do not degrade. They cause the same problems for wildlife as other plastics. Another difficulty is finding land to grow crops for the bioplastic industry. Some people believe that land should be used for growing food not plastic.

60°C (140°F)
Temperature at which bioplastic breaks down

Plastic from Milk

Plastic wrap is used to keep food clean and fresh in stores. Most of the packaging ends up in landfills or in the oceans. Scientists from the U.S. Department of Agriculture are making a new kind of packaging that comes from milk. Their milk-based product is similar to plastic wrap but is not as stretchy. It is both **biodegradable** and **sustainable**. You can eat it too!

Your Turn!

Take a survey of plastics in your home to find out how much you use! You could start with your bedroom or living room, and then work through other rooms in the house like the kitchen, bathroom, and even the garage.

Gather the Evidence

Begin by making a list of all the items you can find that are made from plastic in some way.

- Make tally charts for items of which you have several, such as pens and sports equipment.
- You could take pictures of some of the larger plastic items.
- Perhaps draw a diagram of your room to show where the plastic items are located. You could display this information in a scrapbook or create a poster.

Kitchen utensils are often made of plastic. Which room in your house has the most plastic objects?

Reduce, Reuse, Recycle

Next, look over your results and ask yourself some questions. What are the most common items? How can these items be kept in good shape, reused, and properly recycled? Are there any alternative items you could use that are not made with plastic? How can you reduce the amount of plastic you use? You could brainstorm some ideas with your family or ask your teacher if you can discuss ideas in class. Make a plan to recycle, reuse, or donate plastic items that you no longer need or want. Finally, make it your goal to buy less plastic.

These old plastic bottles have a new life as plant holders! Can you think of other ways to reuse plastic containers?

Glossary

algae Tiny, plant-like organisms

biodegradable Able to break down and become part of the environment

bioplastics Plastics made from plant material

carbon dioxide A gas found naturally in the atmosphere, which is also produced when living things exhale and fuel is burned

decompose Break down into smaller pieces

food chain The order in which living things depend on each other for food

fossil fuels Fuels that are formed from the remains of living things that died millions of years ago

greenhouse gases Gases such as carbon dioxide that build up in the atmosphere and trap heat near Earth

landfill A place where waste materials are buried

microbeads Tiny pieces of plastic used in cosmetics

microplastics Small pieces left over when plastic items break down

plankton Tiny animals and plants that float in the ocean

pollutes Adds something harmful to an environment

properties Characteristics

recycled Made into something different

reduce Use less of a thing

refugees People who flee their country due to unsafe conditions

reuse Use an item again

sustainable Able to be used now and in the future

toxic Poisonous

waste Material that is discarded or no longer used

Find Out More

Books

French, Jess. *What a Waste: Trash, Recycling, and Protecting our Planet*. DK Children, 2019.

Poynter, Dougie. *Plastic Sucks! How YOU Can Make a Difference*. Macmillan Children's Books, 2019.

Rissman, Rebecca. *Reducing, Reusing, and Recycling Waste (Putting the Planet First)*. Crabtree Publishing, 2019.

Websites

Visit the Ocean Conservancy website to find out more about its work, including the international beach cleanup it arranges each year.
oceanconservancy.org/

Find information about plastic, plus an interactive quiz.
www.natgeokids.com/uk/discover/science/general-science/all-about-plastic/

Pictures and information for kids about the problems with plastic.
tiki.oneworld.org/plastic/plastic.html

Index